The Volunteer Management Toolkit (Church Edition)

Resources to Help You Recruit & Retain Volunteers

By Deborah Ike

DEDICATION

To the incredible staff and volunteers whom I've had the
privilege of serving alongside. Your passion and
commitment have instructed and inspired me.

CONTENTS

INTRODUCTION

Over the last ten years, I've been on both sides of the volunteer equation as a volunteer and as a staff member leading volunteers. Experiencing both roles has helped me appreciate the challenges, frustrations, and joys of each group. This toolkit is the culmination of those experiences – both from seeing what's worked really well and what has totally flopped.

Probably one of the biggest tensions I've seen among volunteers is that they are completely conflicted. They want to serve but that desire is stifled by a continual lack of supplies, information or delegated authority. They grow weary when event participants continually ask questions that they can't answer. Their resolve weakens as instructions change depending on whom you talk to or when you talk with them (in the same day, maybe within the same hour!). Frustration sets in when multiple church leaders contact the same volunteer asking him to serve on the same day in different capacities.

However, when I look at the other side of all these frustrations I see volunteer coordinators struggling to meet the demands of the next service or event. They feel like they are constantly begging people to serve, wondering how in the world they're going to manage to make the next service or event happen. Volunteers show up late, or don't show up at all, without any notice or explanation.

In trying to solve these and other problems related to volunteering, we must step back and look at the big picture. From inspiration, to planning and training, we must consider all of the components necessary to continually cultivate a culture of service and gratitude.

I am convinced that the most effective model for leading volunteers is servant-leadership. Practically speaking, this means that in planning the next service opportunity, you should also plan to inspire volunteers, respect their time, ensure they have the information and supplies to succeed, and appreciate their service. If every leader takes the initiative to model our behavior after our Savior who was humble and offered Himself up for us, then our congregations will notice and will want to be a part of the team through volunteer service.

Every volunteer scenario should be a "win-win" for both the church and the volunteer. The church wins in being able to expand its outreach and better serve the congregation; the volunteer wins in developing new relationships with fellow volunteers, leveraging her skills to serve God, and in the opportunity to be part of something bigger than herself. Keep these goals in-mind as you develop your volunteer program. Every communication and volunteer opportunity should reflect these goals.

Here's another thing: Don't apologize for asking people to volunteer. You may not say the exact words, "I apologize" or "I hate to ask, but..." However, you may give the impression that you wish you didn't have to ask for help or that you feel as though you're putting a burden on others. If you truly believe in the vision of your church, thoughtfully plan each volunteer role and opportunity, care about your volunteers as individuals (not just as "worker bees"), and seek to help volunteers connect with each other then you have no reason to apologize. You are doing both your church's congregation and each volunteer a great service, so be confident in your work and view yourself as a connector of people instead of a beggar of people. You are inviting them to be a part of the vision – that's a great invitation to offer and, when communicated and planned well, it is easy to accept.

Recruiting and retaining volunteers is a process that starts before you ever even ask someone to serve. I know it can be very tempting to jump up in the middle of a meeting and throw out a request for volunteers, but 99.9% of the time it will not hurt to plan your work and work your plan. The .1% can then be reserved for life threatening emergencies and you will be more likely to receive a willing response from people who have not been burned out. The process isn't terribly complicated, but it does require planning to lead people through the steps of being recruited to later becoming a leader within your volunteer ranks.

I've designed a four-phased process that you'll lead each volunteer through:

Recruit → Assign → Train → Appreciate

If you've never run a volunteer program before and are starting from scratch, or you've started one and are trying to get some momentum, this can be a daunting task. This toolkit is designed to walk you through these phases along with the specific details of volunteer management from inspiring people, to assigning and training them, as well as recognizing their service. I've included logistical details, templates, and job descriptions. Details may not be your thing, and I understand the desire to simply "do ministry" instead of planning ministry. However, if you'll take the time to plan carefully and pay attention to the details, you'll reap the rewards of a committed and loyal volunteer team. Just remember: These are tools and helpful resources, but your true source of inspiration and strength come from God. Trust Him as you walk through these steps. Pray for wisdom, pray for current and future volunteers, and as you put your hands to the plow, watch God use you for His glory.

There are two types of volunteer service opportunities addressed within this toolkit: weekly services and special events. In this first section, we'll address weekly service volunteers.

SECTION A: WEEKLY SERVICE VOLUNTEERS

CHAPTER 1
RECRUITING VOLUNTEERS

From preparation to actually inviting people to serve

Step 1: Define and Document the Vision

Before you ask anyone to give up their most limited resource, their time, you must be able to communicate a compelling reason for why they should volunteer. People volunteer because they're inspired and want to be part of something bigger than themselves; something that will improve the lives and destiny of others.

As you're working on how to communicate the vision, put yourself in the mind of potential volunteers and answer these questions. (Seriously, get a piece of paper, pretend you're a potential volunteer, and write down your responses to these questions – I'll wait.):

- What is the vision of my church?

- Who will I help?

- How will their lives be different as a result of my efforts?

- What can I contribute (specific skills, abilities, etc.)?

- Who will I be serving alongside?

- What will I learn?

- Will my time and talents be used wisely? How do I know?

- Will they be prepared and have the work planned out in advance?

- Will I have the supplies and equipment needed to do the work well?

- Will they train me?

- How often are they asking me to volunteer?

- How long am I being asked to commit to this volunteer role?

Once you've answered these questions, craft a message to potential volunteers and weave the answers to these questions within the message.

For example:

"At ABC Church we are dedicated to reaching the lost with the Gospel, making disciples and helping hurting people. Our volunteers enable us to achieve this vision at our weekly services by making every person feel welcome and at home as they arrive onto our campus. From the parking lot to the sanctuary, our volunteers are the smiling faces directing traffic, greeting visitors, serving coffee, and seating our guests. ABC Church volunteers also serve in our clothing pantry and food bank, helping struggling families by being the hands and feet of Christ.

We provide the information, training and tools you'll need to be successful. We need volunteers for a variety of roles, so whatever your specific talents, abilities, or time availability, we have a place for you to serve. We'd love for you to join our team of dedicated volunteers. You'll connect with great people and will reap the benefit of knowing that you're following the example of our Savior in serving others."

Now, doesn't that sound better than, "We need your help – please volunteer!"? You'll get a much better response from people if you take the time to develop your message and help each individual see themselves joining the team. It's worth the time and effort involved in developing that message. Take a few minutes to develop your own version of this message (this is important, so don't skip this step!).

Step 2: Identify the Need

Before you ask anyone to volunteer, you also need to know how many people you need and the roles you're asking them to serve in. This information will vary based on the size of your church, number of services you have each week, and the types of programs offered. To help you assess the number of people you will need in each role, I've included the Volunteer Needs Assessment Spreadsheet and Volunteer Organization Chart in this toolkit (see Appendix E). Take a moment to fill out the spreadsheet and then modify the organizational chart to suit your church's needs before moving on to Step 3.

Depending on the size of your congregation, you may need up to 100 (or more) volunteers for each service. If you are the volunteer coordinator for your church, that's a lot of people to manage effectively by yourself. Heed the advice that Jethro gave Moses (Exodus 18:17-23) and appoint leaders to help you. In the Volunteer Needs Assessment, I've included Team Lead roles. The Team Leads should be volunteers who are consistent, dependable members of your church who have proven leadership qualities. Your job is then to provide these Team Leads with the information and supplies they need to be successful. Their role is to pass that information to their teams and keep you informed of how their team is doing, provide feedback and status information to you.

Step 3: Define the roles

If you want to see people lining up to sign up, you've got to define what it is they are signing up for. This means developing a job description for each volunteer role. I know that doesn't sound too exciting, however this is a step you can't afford to skip. Use the job descriptions (see Appendix A for a generic template and Appendix E for a link to download sample job descriptions) included in this toolkit as a starting point and customize each one for your church. The process of developing a job description for each role forces you to think through exactly what you're asking volunteers to do and helps you set expectations with potential volunteers. Documented job descriptions are also useful in making sure that everyone on staff knows the responsibilities of each volunteer role so they can help you identify and recruit new volunteers.

Post these job descriptions on your church website and let people see what would be expected of them if they volunteered for a specific role. Doesn't that mean that they might not volunteer if the job description seems intimidating? Maybe, but do you really want someone to sign up for a role that he is going to quit two weeks later because he didn't know what he was getting himself into? Yeah, I didn't think so.

Step 4: Decide how you're going to have volunteers signup

You need to give careful consideration to how you'll have potential volunteers signup and how you'll gather their information (name, email, phone#, volunteer roles they're interested in, etc.). This part of the process can get tricky (trust me, I've seen it go wrong...fast!). Here are the most common approaches:

1. *Church bulletin insert or card in the seat-back pocket of each chair / pew.* Pros: This is cost effective and requires very little setup. Cons: You may need an interpreter to decipher some people's handwriting - good luck! Also, you'll

need to enter the information into a spreadsheet or church database.

2. *Signup sheets in the lobby or on tables in the back of the sanctuary.* Pros: This is cost effective and requires very little setup. Cons: Again, you may need an interpreter to decipher some people's handwriting. Plus you'll still need to enter the information into a spreadsheet or church database.

3. *Online form via church website.* Pros: First off, this eliminates the handwriting issues. Also, you can integrate the form with your church database, which eliminates the need to enter the data yourself. You can export the list to a spreadsheet (handy if you don't have a database or church management software yet). Finally, there is minimal, if any, cost to this approach depending on your website. Cons: You'll need computers or tablet devices setup so people can signup while at church.

4. *App (available across multiple app stores).* Pros: The pros for this option are the same as the online form approach. Cons: You can't depend solely on an app since not everyone owns a smartphone and can access apps.

I strongly recommend that you go with an online option. This captures the data from each person quickly (and legibly!) and enables you to use either spreadsheets or your church's database if you have one already setup.

The other options can work, but they place more of a burden on church staff and can delay the follow-up process.

Step 5: Design the follow-up process

Notice that all of this is still BEFORE you ask for volunteers! Too many times churches ask for volunteers, do a great job inspiring and motivating people to signup, get a ton of people to volunteer and then, due to the overwhelming response, they lose a large percentage of those potential volunteers because they take too long to follow-up. Save yourself (and your potential volunteers) the hassle and figure this out before you start recruiting.

Here's the great thing about this toolkit – I've already developed a follow-up process for you! Customize it for your church and then run with it.

Follow-up process:

1. *Record* - Enter or upload each applicant's information into your church's database. (If you're just starting out, this might be a spreadsheet. No worries! I've included the Volunteer Information & Assignment Records template for you to use. See Appendix E for details.)

2. *Contact* - Send an email to all volunteers who signed up for children's ministry areas with a link to provide the information needed for a background check and an online volunteer

17

application form (see Appendix B). **Note: If you're doing online signups, you should be able to setup a trigger so when someone indicates that they want to serve in children's ministry, the system will automatically direct them to fill out the application form and background check form. Talk with your website or database administrator about this process.**

3. *Invite* - Call or email all other volunteers based on the area they signed up for and ask them to sign up for an orientation class date (you'll need to have these prescheduled). **Note: If you're doing online signups, you could have the system direct them to signup for an orientation class at that time. You should still follow-up via phone or email to make a personal connection but this function is helpful.**

4. *Train* - Conduct the orientation and training classes.

5. *Host* - The first time a new volunteer arrives to serve, they'll probably feel more comfortable if they're paired with someone who can help show them the ropes. Match each new volunteer up with a seasoned veteran – introduce them and welcome all new volunteers during your pre-service team meeting.

6. *Check-in* - After the service, check-in with the vets to find out how their new friends did that day. Also, check-in sometime that week with

the new volunteers to ask how it went, if they have any questions, etc.

Step 6: Recruit!

Here are five methods for recruiting new volunteers:

1. *Individual Invitations* - Watch for people who are consistent attenders of a specific service, introduce yourself and ask if they would be interested in volunteering at that service.

2. *Ask your current volunteers to recruit their friends.* - If they enjoy volunteering, have established new friendships as a result, grown in their walk with God and have seen how their service has impacted lives, then they will be your best advocates/recruiters. Make sure they're aware of the full process including how to sign up and when the next orientation class will be held so they can relay that to potential volunteers.

3. *Social Media*

   a. Post a call for volunteers on your church's Facebook page. Include a link to your online signup form with the post.

   b. Post information about the orientation class schedule to get people thinking about volunteering.

   c. Send out a tweet from your church's

Twitter account asking for volunteers. Again, include a link to the online signup form.

d. Share stories about volunteer projects, specific volunteer teams, etc. Post pictures (with each individual's permission) of volunteer teams at work and having fun.

4. *Recruiting from the stage*

a. Show video testimonials: Video current volunteers talking about how volunteering has benefited them and their families. Include videos of people who are fairly new to the church talking about how a volunteer made them feel welcome, etc.

b. Share the need: Tell people exactly which areas need the most help.

c. Explain the roles: Briefly describe each role and why it's important.

d. Tell them how to get involved: Explain the signup process and make it easy for people to signup.

e. Tell them what to expect after they sign up: Let them know when to expect a follow-up call or email. Tell them when the next orientation class is scheduled and that this class will provide them with the training they need to be successful.

    f.   Have some fun with this, too! Share funny stories about volunteering, video clips from last year's volunteer appreciation night, video of volunteers serving and smiling, etc. Volunteering really is fun and rewarding, so help people envision themselves in a volunteer position having fun and developing new friendships.

5. *Email / Snail-mail communication* - Include an article within the email and/or print newsletter your church sends out. Let people know where to find more information about the volunteer needs and how to sign up.

CHAPTER 2
ASSIGNING VOLUNTEERS

*Connect each volunteer with a role they are best suited
for and more likely to enjoy*

This part of the process will vary based on the volunteer role. For some roles, there's no need for an interview or background check. Examples may include sorting canned goods at a food pantry, greeting people at the front door before a service, etc. Other roles, however, will require a more involved vetting process. These would include any roles in which a volunteer would be working around minors (children under age eighteen), with money, etc.

Contact people who've expressed interest in roles that require additional review:

1. Ask why the applicant is interested in that particular opportunity. Does she have experience working with children? Is he good with numbers? Get a sense of why this person wants to serve and what he/she can bring to the team.

2. Ask the applicant to complete the background check form and volunteer application (if he hasn't done so already).

3. While you're waiting for the background check results, contact the applicant's references. If the check comes out clean and the references check out, proceed to the next step, which is training.

CHAPTER 3
TRAINING VOLUNTEERS

Set them up to win from the start

Training will vary based on the role. Sorting canned goods or clothing likely just requires a 10-15 minute briefing when a team of volunteers arrives on-site. Ushering, working in the coffee bar or bookstore requires a bit more instruction, while working around children requires a more detailed level of training for safety purposes. Regardless of the training needed, here's how to proceed once an applicant is assigned to a specific role.

Step 1: Schedule for training

Schedule the volunteer to attend the next available volunteer orientation and training breakout for that role. Automate this process as much as possible. If you have a church database system, it may include functionality to email volunteers with a calendar invite so they can quickly add the orientation class to their calendar regardless of platform – Apple, PC, Google Calendar, etc. In addition, schedule an email to go out to everyone who has signed up for a class 1-2 days prior to the class as a reminder.

Step 2: Conduct the orientation and training

Orientation & Training Agenda

Main Session – This session is for all new volunteers. Your goal here is to welcome them to the team and set the overall guidelines/expectations that apply across the board.

Time Required: 30 minutes

Materials: One-page handout with the guidelines and expectations that your church has of its volunteers (see Appendix C for a sample handout).

Presentation: Welcome everyone and thank them for their interest in volunteering with your church. Reiterate the vision and review the guidelines and expectations handout. Announce that the next step is to attend the breakout training session for their volunteer role. Let them know where each session is located (which room/area) and dismiss them to their session. They should know which session to attend based on your follow-up with them. However, if someone isn't sure where to go, have the list of volunteers and which session they're scheduled to attend ready to direct volunteers to the right place.

<u>Breakout Training Sessions:</u> Divide them up into breakout sessions by area (Welcome Hosts, Ushers, Bookstore, etc.) and train each group on its specific responsibilities. Remind them of the job description and why that particular role is important (again, keeping the vision in front of them at all times is key). Let them know which services you need the most volunteers for and at the end, ask them to commit to a service for a certain number of months. Also, let them know that, if after the session they're not sure that this role is right for them, you'd love to talk with them about which role might be a better fit. You want each person serving in a role that they'll enjoy, be able to commit to, and will feel like they're making a great contribution in.

<u>Socialize:</u> When each breakout-training session concludes, have coffee/water/snacks at the back of the room and encourage people to stick around for a while to chat. Mingle through the crowd, introducing yourself to new volunteers and getting to know them. Include your volunteer team leads in this as well. Remember: This is not as much about filling volunteer roles as it is about connecting people. If you'll connect with them, the volunteer roles will be filled.

Step 3: Get started

Schedule each volunteer's first day and assign him/her to a veteran volunteer (someone who has been serving for at least six months). Send out a reminder email 1-2 days prior to their first service day and let them know what time to arrive, where to go, and who to connect with when they arrive (this should be the veteran volunteer).

Let them know that they'll shadow a veteran. That'll help alleviate any anxiety they may have about the first day.

Step 4: First Day Introductions

On each volunteer's first day, introduce him/her to the team and to the veteran volunteer who has been assigned to them. Afterwards, follow-up with both the new volunteer and the veteran (separately) to ask how it went. Address any concerns immediately.

Send a thank you note to each new volunteer within one week, letting them know that you're happy to have them on the team and to let you know if they have any questions. **If you have a lot of new volunteers (first of all, yea!), ask your volunteer team leads to write some of the cards for the new volunteers that were added to their teams. Provide them with the cards (with the envelope already addressed to the volunteer) and stamps.**

CHAPTER 4
APPRECIATING YOUR VOLUNTEERS

Mom was right. Saying "please" and "thank you" are always in-style.

Your volunteers are giving you their talents, abilities and their time. If you take them for granted, forget to encourage and inspire, or don't listen to their input, they will leave. Even the most dedicated volunteer will get burned out and tired of dealing with constant changes or lack of preparation.

How to show volunteers you appreciate them:

1. *Respect their time.* Tell them when they need to arrive (then start on time) and when they'll be done (and finish on time).

2. *Plan the work.* Always be prepared and have the supplies, information and instructions they'll

need ready before they arrive. Don't ask them to come in for a special meeting, training, or to help with a special project or event without being fully prepared for them.

3. *Mail hand-written thank you notes to volunteers* (2-3 each week is certainly doable). In the note, be specific about what you appreciate about that volunteer, not just a generic "thanks for serving".

4. *Praise* a specific volunteer or volunteer team during a service.

5. *Organize a lunch outing with your volunteer team after a Sunday service* (everyone can pay for their own meal, but at least make the reservations and get the conversation going). This is a great chance to get to know your volunteers.

6. *Host a volunteer appreciation night 1-2 times each year.* Go out to the movies, go bowling, cater in dessert and coffee at the church, etc.

7. *Recognize important dates in your volunteers' lives* such as wedding anniversaries, birthdays, or service anniversaries (6 months, 1 year, 5 years, etc.). Send them a card or email, announce service anniversaries on your church's Facebook page, on Twitter, or mention it during a pre-service team meeting.

8. *Meet with your volunteer leaders 4-6 times per*

year. Serve coffee and snacks. Share any upcoming changes, announcements, etc. Ask for feedback, ideas for improvement, concerns, what they like / don't like, etc.

9. *Listen.* Walk around and chat with your volunteers. Get to know them. Ask about their kids, hobbies, pets, work, church experiences, etc.

10. *Pray for your volunteers during the week.* Pray for them as a group and individually.

11. *Disciple your volunteers.* Include an encouraging word with your weekly announcement email. Share a verse that has really captured your attention lately. Encourage them to study the Bible. Recommend a great book by a Christian author that you've read recently.

12. *Communicate.* Setup an email distribution list for each volunteer team and email them as needed with new announcements, upcoming changes, etc. Use social media or group text messaging as well. The key is to ask your volunteers what communication method works best for them. You may get a few different answers, but that information will help you reach them more effectively.

13. *Say thank you.* Tell them how much you appreciate their faithfulness to serve on a

consistent basis.

14. *Share testimonies.* As you hear people express how volunteers helped them feel welcome, answered their questions, prayed with them, encouraged their kids, etc. share those stories with your teams. Those are specific instances you can relate of people whose lives they've impacted – which are really why people volunteer (and why they keep volunteering).

SECTION B: SPECIAL EVENT VOLUNTEERS

CHAPTER 5
RECRUITING SPECIAL EVENT VOLUNTEERS

*Volunteering for a special event is a great way for
people to test the waters*

Recruiting and retaining volunteers for a special event is a bit different than for weekly services. In many cases, this is an opportunity for someone to serve for the first time which could then lead to them becoming a part of your volunteer team for a weekly service. In other words, this is a first impression for many of what it's like to volunteer for your church so don't mess this up!

Step 1: Define and Document the Vision

Inspiration is just as important for a one-time event as it is for a weekly service. You must be able to communicate why you're doing this event, who you're trying to reach (students, marrieds, singles, kids, unchurched, etc.), and how this event will accomplish that goal. Take a few minutes to answer these questions from the viewpoint of a potential volunteer.

- What is the vision of this event?

- Who will I help?

- How will their lives be different as a result of my efforts?

- What can I contribute (specific skills, abilities, etc.)?

- Who will I be serving alongside?

- What will I learn?

- Will my time and talents be used wisely? How do I know?

- Will they be prepared and have the work planned out in advance?

- Will I have the supplies and equipment needed to do the work well?

- Will they train me?

- What is the schedule for this event? Are they asking me to be there the whole time or for a specific shift?

Once you've answered these questions, craft a message to potential volunteers and weave the answers to these questions within the message.

Step 2: Identify the need

Before you ask anyone to volunteer, you also need to

know how many people you need and the roles you're asking them to serve in. This information will vary based on the event type and size. To help you assess the number of people you will need in each role, I've included the Special Event Volunteer Needs Assessment Spreadsheet and Special Event Volunteer Organization. Take a moment and fill out the spreadsheet and then modify the organizational chart to suit your church's needs before moving on to the next step.

Step 3: Define the roles

Explain exactly what you're looking for from volunteers for this event.

- Do you need people to handle ticket sales?

- Crowd control?

- Food preparation and serving?

- Merchandise sales?

- Stage / production setup and tear down?

- Registration?

There are special event job descriptions (see Appendix E) for a variety of roles included in this toolkit – start with these and customize them for your event. By letting potential volunteers know what you need and expect, you'll help people self-select themselves out of the wrong roles and into the right ones.

Step 4: Decide how you're going to have volunteers sign up

Again, please give careful consideration to how you'll have potential volunteers signup and how you'll gather their information. Here are the most common approaches:

1. *Church bulletin insert or card in the seat-back pocket of each chair / pew.* Pros: This is cost effective and requires very little setup. Cons: You may need an interpreter to decipher some people's handwriting - good luck! Also, you'll need to enter the information into a spreadsheet or church database.

2. *Signup sheets in the lobby or on tables in the back of the sanctuary.* Pros: This is cost effective and requires very little setup. Cons: Again, you may need an interpreter to decipher some people's handwriting. Plus you'll still need to enter the information into a spreadsheet or church database.

3. *Online form via church website.* Pros: First off, this eliminates the handwriting issues. Also, you can integrate the form with your church database which eliminates the need to enter the data yourself. You can export the list to a spreadsheet (handy if you don't have a database or church management software yet). Finally, there is minimal, if any, cost to this approach depending on your website. Cons: You'll need

computers or tablet devices setup so people can signup while at church.

4. *App (available across multiple app stores).* Pros: The pros for this option are the same as the online form approach. Cons: You can't depend solely on an apps since not everyone owns a smartphone and can access apps.

I strongly recommend that you go with an online option. This captures the data from each person quickly (and legibly!), enables you to use either spreadsheets or your church's database if you have one already setup. The other options can work, but they place more of a burden on church staff and can delay the follow-up process.

Step 5: Design the follow up process

Again, notice that this is BEFORE you ask for volunteers!

Follow-up process:

1. *Record* - Enter applicant's information into your church's database. (If you're just starting out, this might be a spreadsheet. No worries! I've included the Volunteer Information & Assignment Records-Special Events for you to use. See Appendix E for details.)

2. *Contact* - Email or call those who've signed up to confirm where and when they're serving at the event and if they need to attend training. If training is required for their role at the event, include options of days/times for them to attend

training and ask them to sign up for one of those training options. **Note: If you're doing online signups, you could have the system direct them to signup for an orientation class at that time. You should still follow-up via phone or email to make a personal connection but this function is helpful.**

3. *Train* - Conduct training as needed.

Step 6: Recruit

Here are several methods to use in recruiting for a special event:

1. *Recruit individuals for leadership roles or roles requiring a special skillset.* - Before you begin contacting people, have the leaders who will be recruiting submit their wish list of names and corresponding roles for the volunteers in their area. Compile that into the Volunteer Information & Assignment Records-Special Events spreadsheet and look for duplicates (people that are about to be asked to fill multiple roles for the same event). Figure out which role you're going to recruit each person for (only ONE!) and then inform your leaders of any necessary changes so they can start making those calls.

2. *Social Media*

   a. Post a call for volunteers on your church's Facebook page. Include a link to your online signup form with the post.

b. Post information about the orientation class schedule to get people thinking about volunteering.

c. Send out a tweet from your church's Twitter account asking for volunteers. Again, include a link to the online signup form.

d. Share stories about volunteers from other events (from the same event the prior year, if possible).

3. *Recruiting from the stage*

a. Show video testimonials: Video current volunteers talking about how volunteering has benefited them and their families. Include videos of people who are fairly new to the church talking about how a volunteer made them feel welcome, etc.

b. Share the need: Communicate why your church is hosting this event, why it's important and how you need volunteers to participate.

c. Explain the roles: Briefly describe each role and why it's important.

d. Tell them how to get involved: Explain the signup process and make it easy for people to signup.

    e. Tell them what to expect after they sign up: Let them know when to expect a follow-up call or email.

4. *Email / Snail-mail communication* - Include an article within the email and/or print newsletter your church sends out leading up to the event. Let people know where to find more information about the volunteer needs and how to sign up.

CHAPTER 6
ASSIGNING VOLUNTEERS FOR SPECIAL EVENTS

As you're recruiting and people are signing up for specific roles, email and/or call people to confirm which role and at what day/time they're serving. Also let them know if they need to attend a training class before the event. If training is required, ask them to sign up for a training session (you may need to schedule a few so that people can fit one into their schedule).

CHAPTER 7
TRAINING VOLUNTEERS FOR SPECIAL EVENTS

It may just be for one day, but they still need to know what you expect.

The level of training required will vary by role. Regardless of how you train your volunteers, send them instructions before the event (provide a document with the instructions at the training session and send it to them prior to the event).

The day of the event, go over the instructions even if they've already attended a training session (people forget or don't read the instructions). The instructions should include:

Timing: What time volunteers should arrive and the time they can expect to be done.

Attire: What they should wear, whether they need to wear a specific volunteer t-shirt and shorts/jeans or something dressier. This is covered in the job descriptions, but reiterate within the instructions.

Meals: For longer events, let volunteers know if the church will provide for their meals, if food vendors will be on-site, or if they'll need to make other arrangements.

Location: Let volunteers know where to meet when they arrive. Let them know if they need to check-in and whom they are meeting.

Also, make sure you plan ahead and have everything they'll need to be successful ready for them. This includes supplies such as pens, pencils, forms, clipboards, tickets, water, t-shirts, event schedule, maps, etc.

Remember: Your success and the success of your event is directly tied to the success of your volunteers. If they win, you win – so make sure they're set up to win!

CHAPTER 8
APPRECIATING SPECIAL EVENT VOLUNTEERS

You couldn't have pulled off the event without them.

Appreciating at the Event:

When your volunteers arrive and before you dive into the instructions for the day, thank them for coming to serve and remind them of why their service is so important and what you're collectively accomplishing through the event. Then review the instructions and answer any questions. Before you release them to get started, pray with your team to start the day off right.

Check in with your team throughout the event. Stay nearby to answer their questions, ask if there's anything they need (and get it for them ASAP), take their place for a few minutes so they can take a break, etc. At the end of their shift or of the event, whichever comes first; thank each person for their help.

Appreciating after the Event:

Mail thank you cards to each volunteer within one week of the event

Within 1-2 weeks after a big event, facilitate a lessons learned session with your volunteers. You don't have to pull everyone in if it's a large group, but ask 10-15 volunteer leaders to come in and share their feedback. Ask what went well and what needs to be improved for the next event. Serve coffee and a few snacks (providing food and caffeine are signs of a gracious host). Have someone assigned to take notes (NOT a volunteer!) and someone else to facilitate the discussion. Don't be defensive when they point out what went wrong – listen and ask questions if you're not clear on what they're saying. Ask for suggestions on how to improve or fix that particular problem.

If you had fifty or more volunteers at an event, send out a survey to ask them how it went. You can use an online tool such as SurveyMonkey for little to no cost. I've also included a sample survey in Appendix D. As part of the survey, you'll notice that one of the questions provides each volunteer with the opportunity to sign up for a service volunteer role. This capitalizes on what was hopefully a great volunteer experience and gets them thinking about possibly joining a weekly service volunteer team.

Document the lessons learned and discuss them with your church staff. Identify what needs to be changed, put a plan in place to make those changes (including a deadline for each change), and hold each other accountable to implementing the changes by the deadlines. Please note that it is extremely frustrating and discouraging to your volunteers if they provide you with feedback that is never considered or acted upon. What's really great is when you implement one of their suggestions and then publicly thank them for their idea and feedback once its implemented!

CONCLUSION

At this point, I hope you're feeling well equipped to launch or revamp your volunteer program. If you're feeling overwhelmed, take a deep breath and pray. You'll be fine. Just take this one step at a time, implement these processes and seek out feedback from people you trust. The most rewarding aspect of coordinating volunteers is when you see them connecting with each other and with visitors. That's what this is all about, really – making connections so that the Body of Christ can work together. You get to help facilitate those connections and while all the details involved may be stressful at times, you can truly do all things through Christ who strengthens you. Don't try to do this in your own strength; that will backfire quickly. Trust God, work diligently, connect people and your efforts will bear much fruit.

If you need assistance in implementing these steps or would like an evaluation of your volunteer program, contact me at www.velocityministrymanagement.com.

My Volunteer Management Assessment & Coaching Program is designed to assess and then walk with you through implementing recommended changes to further improve your program.

ABOUT THE AUTHOR

Deborah Ike (formerly Wipf) is the President & Founder of Velocity Ministry Management, a company dedicated to vision implementation for church leaders.

In addition to serving in ministry, Deborah has worked in the corporate arena to discover how to leverage business principles for ministry vision. She worked for an international consulting firm and a Fortune 500 company doing consulting, project management, and risk management.

Deborah is certified as a Project Management Professional (PMP) through the Project Management Institute. She's the author of The Volunteer Management Toolkit (Church Edition) and you can find her articles on sites such as WorshipFacilities.com, Pastors.com, XPastor.org, and via The Church Network.

For more information, you can find Deborah online at:

www.velocityministrymanagement.com

Twitter: @DeborahIkeVMM

Facebook:
www.facebook.com/velocityministrymgmt

APPENDIX A: JOB DESCRIPTION TEMPLATE

Job Title

Organization Name

What we do

Brief description of the purpose for this volunteer role.

Specific expectations

List of expectations including when volunteers should arrive, what they need to do, how long they need to stay at this role at each service, etc.

Attire

List your expectations for attire. Do they need to wear volunteer t-shirts or regular church attire? What does "regular church attire" look like for your church? Provide volunteers with that information in this section.

For the complete MS Word file of job descriptions for weekly service and special event volunteers, go to http://www.velocityministrymanagement.com/home/the-volunteer-management-toolkit-church-edition-resources-page/.

APPENDIX B: VOLUNTEER APPLICATION FORM

First Name:		Last Name:	
Email:		Phone:	
Address:		City, State & Zip Code:	

I'm interested in volunteering in these areas (check all that apply):

Welcome Host / Greeter

Usher / Seater

Parking Attendant

Bookstore

Coffee bar

Children's Ministry (Please note that a background check and three references are required for serving in any of the Children's Ministry areas)

I'm interested in volunteering at these services (check all that apply):

Sunday Service A

Sunday Service B

Wednesday Service

APPENDIX C: SAMPLE VOLUNTEER ORIENTATION CLASS HANDOUT

Welcome! Thank you for joining the team and volunteering with ABC Church. We are excited to connect you with our staff and veteran volunteers.

Here are a few key things we thought you'd want to know before we get started:

Today's agenda:

After this quick orientation session, we'll split up based on the volunteer area you're joining to provide you with the specific training for that area.

Once training has concluded, you're invited to join us for snacks and a chance to get to know each other.

Our staff, volunteer team leaders and veteran volunteers are here to help you and to answer any questions you may have. Please don't hesitate to ask.

We love our volunteers! We recognize that you have busy lives and lots to do, so the fact that you want to serve with us is wonderful. We value your time and constantly strive to ensure that you have the information and supplies needed to be effective. If at any time it seems like we've missed something, please let us know.

We work as unto the Lord which means excellence in everything. We're not expecting perfection, but we do strive for excellence. We'll discuss this in more detail at the training sessions, but overall this means that we arrive and finish on time, we dress appropriately, and we treat each other and every guest with sincere kindness.

APPENDIX D:
SAMPLE SURVEY TO USE AFTER A SPECIAL EVENT

Introduction: Thank you for volunteering at our ABC Event last week! Your hard work and dedication helped make this event a great success. We're always seeking to improve our events and communication with volunteers.

Please complete the following survey to help us improve.

1. I had all the information needed to be successful at my role during the event.
   a. True
   b. False (Please tell us what additional information would have been helpful):
2. I had all the supplies needed to be successful at my role during the event.
   a. True
   b. False (Please tell us what additional supplies would have been helpful):
3. I received a reminder the week prior to the event.
   a. Yes
   b. No
4. A Team Lead or Staff Member was available to answer questions during the event.
   a. Yes
   b. No
5. Did you hear any complaints or frustrations

expressed by event participants?

    a. Yes (If yes, please describe what you heard):

    b. No

6. Did you hear any specific compliments expressed by event participants?

    a. Yes (If yes, please describe what you heard):

    b. No

7. Is there anything we could have done differently that would have made your job easier or more effective? If so, please include that information in the comments:

8. If you are not currently volunteering at a weekly service, would you be interested in doing so?

    a. Yes

    b. No

    c. N/A – I'm already volunteering at a weekly service.

APPENDIX E: TOOLKIT RESOURCES

To download the following items, go to http://www.velocityministrymanagement.com/home/the-volunteer-management-toolkit-church-edition-resources-page/.

- Volunteer Organization Chart

- Volunteer Job Descriptions

- Volunteer Needs Assessment Spreadsheet Template

- Volunteer Information & Assignment Records Spreadsheet Template

Made in the USA
Middletown, DE
29 August 2018